What they don't tell you about

WORLD WAR II

By Bob Fowke

Dedicated to all the brave people
who fought the Nazis.

Hello, my name's Linda Hand. I'm a Land Army girl. We helped farmers to produce food during the dark dangerous days of World War II. Come with me and we'll find out what war meant for ordinary people, as well as for the generals and politicians.

Published in 2013 by Wayland

Text and illustrations copyright © Bob Fowke 2013

Wayland
338 Euston Road
London NW1 3BH

Wayland Australia
Level 17/207 Kent Street
Sydney, NSW 2000

Produced for Wayland by Bob Fowke & Co
Cover design: Lisa Peacock
Cover illustration: Nick Hardcastle

A CIP catalogue record for this book is available from the British Library.

ISBN 978 0 7502 8047 1

10 9 8 7 6 5 4 3 2 1

Printed and bound by CPI Group (UK) Ltd, Croydon, CR0 4YY

First published in 2001 by Hodder Children's Books

Wayland is a division of Hachette Children's Books, an Hachette UK Company
www.hachette.co.uk

CONTENTS

🦶 Watch out for the *Sign of the Foot*! Whenever you see this sign in the book it means there are some more details at the *FOOT* of the page, like here.

DOODLE-BUG!

BEWARE BUZZ-BOMBS.

First of all, let's find out what life was like on the street.

MUMBLE MUMBLE...   GRUMBLE?

ARTHUR CA...

ONE QUIET AFTERNOON ...

London, August 1944. Two women step out of a greengrocer's shop with bags of shopping and their hair in curlers, their clothes clean but shabby. A workman climbs out of a hole in the road where he's been working. No one's in a rush, and all seems peaceful as a snooze in the park.

There's just a bit of a noise in the sky above. It sounds something like a cheap motorbike in need of a service.

Nobody seems to take any notice.

Then the motorbike-noise cuts out. The two women calmly step back into the grocer's shop and the workman slips back into his hole.

Next moment there's a rush of wind and a loud bomb-explosion somewhere close, followed by the clatter of bricks and glass on tarmac. Then the two women come out of the grocer's, still chatting, and the workman pops out of his hole. Life goes on.

Bombs were frightening. But in the summer of 1944 the brave people who stayed in London had learned to put up with them.

BUZZ OFF!

The bomb with the noisy engine was called a V1 flying bomb, also known as a 'doodle-bug' or 'buzz-bomb'. They flew at about 640 kph, but it was only when the engine stopped that you had to worry. No engine noise meant that a V1 was about to plunge to earth. It wasn't a good idea to be underneath when it did.

Doodle-bugs were designed to cause maximum havoc. Like all bombs, they killed and wounded people and destroyed their homes.

World War II had been going on for five years by the summer of 1944, and millions of people all over the world had died because of it. The British had got used to living in fear of death during bombing campaigns. And as well as bombs they had got used to a lot of other things, like not having much food for instance, or having to patch up their old clothes.

War had become a way of life.

But at least by 1944 they were winning - it wasn't like that at first.

BULLY FOR YOU!

OR - WHO STARTED IT?

> Germany lost World War I in 1918. Millions had died. It was called the 'war that will end war'. Britain, France and Russia had been Germany's main enemies.

WELL, THAT SHOULD DO IT.

I'VE HAD ENOUGH OF THIS!

FANCY ANOTHER ONE?

World War II started just twenty-one years after the end of World War I and it was even bigger. It spread out from Europe like a cancer until most of the world was fighting. On one side were Britain, France, the countries of the British Empire, and other allies of the British. (The Americans joined the British later.) On the other side were Germany, Japan, and Italy and their allies. The German side were called the 'Axis Powers', the British side were called the 'Allies'.

Allies are a bit like friends. Countries which are *allied* to each other will fight on the same side during a war.

HOW IT ALL BEGAN

Back in 1939 when World War II started, Britain was a world super-power - just as America is today, but more so in some ways. The British Empire included India, Pakistan, half of Africa, Australia, New Zealand, Canada, Hong Kong and Singapore, plus other countries.

Britain was rich and powerful, but her army was quite small and out-of-date. Greedy eyes were watching her.

POOR OLD GERMANS

It was the Germans who were the biggest problem.

After the German defeat at the end of the First World War the German Ruhr region had been run by the French.

Millions of Germans lived in land governed by Poles, Czechs or Russians.

In the 1920s German money lost its value, causing great suffering. You needed so much money to buy the simplest things that people would sometimes take their money to the shop in a wheelbarrow.

Millions of workers around the world had become unemployed during the Great Depression in the 1930s. Germans suffered more than most.

In 1933 the Germans found a new leader who they hoped would solve their problems. His name was *Adolf Hitler*.

ADOLF SCHICKELGRUBER - NEVER HEARD OF HIM!

In 1876 a small-time Austrian customs official called Schickelgruber changed his name to Hitler. Then in 1889 he and his wife had a baby son whom they called Adolf. No one could have guessed that this baby would grow up to be one of the most evil men who has ever lived.

Young Adolf wanted to be a great artist, but he wasn't good enough. Unfortunately he had another hobby - politics. In 1919, having moved to Germany, he became the seventh member of the tiny National Socialist German Workers' Party - or Nazis for short. From then on politics stopped being a hobby and became a way of life.

There was no stopping him. He turned out to be a political genius, becoming first leader of the Nazi Party and then, in 1933, Chancellor of all Germany, by which time his Nazi Party had thousands of members.

The world was going to have to take notice of Adolf Schickelgruber/Hitler.

The German *Chancellor* does the same sort of job as the British Prime Minister.

WHICH IS THE REAL HITLER?

Adolf Hitler was a very evil man. Like many evil men he could seem kind and jolly to his friends and family if he wanted to. In fact, like many dangerous men, he would never have been able to cause as much suffering as he did, if a lot of people hadn't been fooled by him.

VEGETARIAN.

LOVES CHILDREN.

LIKES PAINTING WATERCOLOURS.

LOVES POWER.

RACIST.

BAD IDEAS

Hitler's Party came to power with some dangerous ideas which were bound to cause trouble. Here are some of them:

Unfortunately Hitler seemed to sort out the German economy in no time. He started a massive programme to build guns, warships, planes and tanks, which meant that most men had a job, for a while. He introduced a housing scheme, motorways, equal pay for women, and better family allowances. He promised that everyone would have a house of their own and a car. Many Germans felt better off than at any time since World War I.

Although many Germans felt better off, a lot of them didn't but kept quiet about it.

Even before gaining power the Nazis had learned how to frighten people who disagreed with them. They staged huge, terrifying, political demonstrations and attacked their enemies on the streets.

Soon only a few very brave people dared to stand up to them.

THE MASTER RACE

The Nazis believed that Germans, or rather *Aryans* (a word which included some other north-Europeans), were the *Master Race*. Members of the Master Race were meant to have fair hair and blue eyes if possible. It was their duty to rule the world. And their empire would last a thousand years.

The Nazis realised that there weren't enough members of the Master Race to rule everywhere immediately, so the first duty of German women was to have lots of children. Women who left work to marry were paid special marriage vouchers worth an average eight months' wages. They might be awarded the 'Mothers' Cross' if they had a lot of children. Divorce, birth-control, abortion and homosexuality were all made illegal because they stopped women from having as many babies as possible. Soon there were lots of blue-eyed babies.

From the very beginning the Nazis wanted Germany to be 'racially pure'. There was no room in their

Germany for Jews or gypsies or anyone who opposed them. So all these other people were allowed to have as many divorces and abortions as they wanted. But of course legal abortions and divorce wouldn't altogether stop these people having children: huge prisons or 'concentration camps' for unwanted people were bound to result from Nazi ideas.

So what about other countries? Well other races were meant to serve the Master Race. Once the Germans ruled the world these other races would be specially bred to make good servants and workers.

It all sounds like madness now. As Hitler's right-hand man, Joseph Goebbels, admitted at the time: *'If the German people had known what the Nazi Party intended to do once it gained power, they would never have voted for it'*.

But fortunately for the Nazis, and unfortunately for the rest of the world, the Germans didn't know what the Nazi Party intended - and a lot of them *did* vote for it - as long as Hitler let them vote.

Hitler had become Chancellor in 1932 after winning an election. By the summer of 1933 he had crushed all the opposition political parties. And in 1934 he became both Chancellor and President of Germany at the same time. From then on he became known as the *Reichs Chancellor* or *Fuhrer*, which means 'leader'. There would be no more elections to the German *Reichstag*, or parliament, as long as the *Fuhrer* was in power.

FASCIST FACTS

The German Nazis were fascists. In a fascist state people are meant to obey their rulers without question. Those who disobey are punished ruthlessly, and there's no voting for a change of government.

Fascists are extreme nationalists, meaning they want their own country to have as much power as possible, normally at the expense of other countries. They usually hate people of other races, especially if people of other races share their country with them.

The first fascist party was started in 1919 in Italy. Its leader was a blacksmith's son called Benito Mussolini.

Mussolini

The Italian fascists planned to build a new Roman Empire, and the word *fascist* comes from the Latin word *fasces* for the bundles of rods with an axe sticking out which were carried on ancient Roman state processions. Italian fascist thugs were known as 'black-shirts' from their uniform.

GRUESOME GALLERY

A noxious nest of nasty Nazis.

 GOEBBELS

Dr Joseph Goebbels was in charge of all Nazi publicity. As editor of the newspaper *Der Angriff*, he whipped up hatred of Jews and Communists. He and his wife killed themselves and their six children in 1945.

GOERING

An ex-World War I fighter-pilot and art-lover who looted the museums of Europe of their treasures, Hermann Goering was head of the German air force and became for a while the second most powerful Nazi after Hitler. He poisoned himself in 1946, on the eve of his execution.

HEYDRICH

Reinhard Heydrich was head of the German security services and hideously cruel. He wrote the first draft of *The Final Solution to the Jewish Problem* which argued for the mass-murder of Jews.

SPEER

Albert Speer was an architect turned Nazi who rose to control German industry during the War. He was sentenced to twenty years in prison after the War for his use of slave labour.

STREICHER

A vicious Nazi hate-monger, Julius Streicher staged the massive Nuremberg Rallies. Found guilty of corruption, he retired to his farm in 1940. He was executed for war crimes in 1946.

OLYMPIC GAMES STORY

In August 1936 the Olympic Games were held in Berlin, the capital of Germany. Here was a great opportunity to prove to the world that the Master Race were best at athletics. The stadium held a massive 110,000 crowd from all over the world.

Unfortunately for the Nazis, the star of the games was Jesse Owens, who won the gold medals for the hundred metres and the two hundred metres. Jesse was a black American - nothing like a member of the Master Race!

Hitler was very angry to see Jesse beat his German athletes - so angry that during the medal awards ceremony he refused to shake Jesse's hand and then left the stadium.

THOUSAND-YEAR REICH

The Nazis called their hoped-for empire the *Thousand-Year Reich*. They planned to have colonies of conquered people working for them all over the world, and they planned how they would rule them. During the Second World War, whenever they conquered a new country they put their ideas into practice.

 Jews and other 'undesirables', such as gypsies, homosexuals and communists, were sent to concentration camps to be worked to death.

 Able-bodied men from Eastern Europe were used as slave labour in German factories (the *Volkswagen* company used lots of slave labour).

 Conquered lands were ruled by provincial governors who were as powerful as little kings in their own areas. The provincial governors were very brutal Nazis. They made many extra enemies for the Germans.

SS - SERIOUSLY SINISTER

To make sure the provincial governors obeyed orders from Germany they were watched by a special force of Nazis known as the *SS* . These were meant to be the cream of the Master Race. It was said that they were so perfect that even if a man had a filling in his tooth he couldn't join them.

Hitler planned that the SS would be the power-house of his new empire. They were trained to be completely ruthless in enforcing Nazi ideas. So if an SS man was in command of a concentration camp he could be

SS stands for *Schutzstaffel*, meaning 'protection squadron'.

horribly brutal to the prisoners without feeling bad about it. After all, according to Nazi ideas, by killing prisoners he was helping to 'cleanse' Germany of her enemies.

SPACE RACE

Hitler wanted to breed more members of the Master Race to run his empire, but at the same time he believed there wasn't enough land in Germany for members of the Master Race already living in it. He thought they needed living space.

The first task was to gather all Germans together into one country.

March 1936. German troops march into the Rhineland in Southern Germany, forbidden to them since World War I.

March 1938. Austria, which has a population of over six million German-speakers, taken over by Germany in an operation known as the *Anschluss*.

September 1938. At a meeting in Munich, the British Prime Minister, Neville Chamberlain, agrees that Germany can take over the Sudetenland in Czechoslovakia, home to three million Germans.

The next task was to grab more living space. Hitler wanted to take it from Eastern Europe.

March 1939. German troops invade the rest of Czechoslovakia. Britain and France do not interfere.

In September 1939 German troops (and their Russian allies) attack Poland. But this time Hitler has gone too far. After all, who might he invade next? France and Britain declare war on Germany.

World War II has begun - only twenty-one years after World War I has ended. Ordinary Germans are no happier about it than the British or French.

WHAT'S ALL THE FUSS ABOUT?

THE PHONEY WAR.

As soon as it had declared war on Germany, the British Parliament passed a law saying that all men between the ages of eighteen and forty-one had to join the army, navy or air force if they were asked to.

MAD BLIND VICARS NOT WANTED

Only a handful could avoid military service:

People certified mad.

Vicars and other clergymen.

Blind people.

People with jobs in 'reserved occupations'. These were jobs which were vital for the war effort, such as mining and farming.

A small number of men were pacifists. This meant that they didn't believe in war, even against the evil of  the Nazis. These people were called 'conscientious objectors'. They still had to join the armed services if they were asked, but in non-fighting jobs such as ambulance driver.

All right Tom?

Men flocked to join the army. Between May and December 1939, 761,600 men and 31,960 women joined up. Most of them had never been soldiers before - and would never want to be soldiers again once the War was over.

New 'Tommies', as British soldiers were called, got a short haircut, a new uniform (which was rough and itchy till you got used to it) and fourteen weeks' training, which mainly involved marching around and learning to shoot their weapons. Here are some of them:

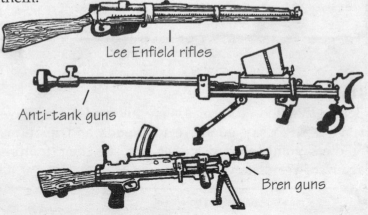

Lee Enfield rifles

Anti-tank guns

Bren guns

Then, with their new weapons and uniforms, the soldiers were packed off to France to wait for the Germans.

MAD MOBILE MINE

Throughout the War rival armies raced to invent new and more deadly weapons. In 1940 King Haakon VII of Norway was chased across Roehampton golf links by a demonstration 'mobile mine' which had run out of control. He was saved when its wheels got stuck in a bunker!

IT'S NO HOLIDAY

Before they left, Tommies were allowed a few days' leave 🦶 to say goodbye to friends and relations. Soldiers going abroad might not see their families again for years, if ever.

Leave means permission to be absent.

For those who went abroad, everything seemed very different from England. It was the first time most of them had been away and they weren't ready for it. As one soldier said of the French:

'They have eggs but they don't fry them properly, they cook them. Bread they give you in big chunks. Tea they cannot make at all, and I didn't like the coffee.'

Once abroad their only contact with home was by post. Letters from home were more precious than gold. The Government understood how important letters were, and it made sure that postage from England took only about three days, even in battle conditions. The army postmen worked hard: during Christmas 1939 they delivered vast quantities of parcels and letters.

ANYTHING FOR ME?

DON'T SUPPOSE SO MATE.

Letters were censored in case enemy spies got hold of them - meaning that the letters were read by an officer to make sure they didn't give away any secrets. Tommies could send an uncensored 'Field Service Postcard', but all that said was the date, address and name of sender to show he was still alive.

When the Tommies got to France there was nothing much to do at first. Fortunately the army believed in

keeping its soldiers fit and healthy:
each battalion had fifty
kilograms of sports gear,
including twenty-four
hockey sticks, fifty pairs
of football boots and strip
enough for six teams.

DOWN ON THE FARM

At the same time as the army of Tommies was leaving for France, another army was leaving home - for the countryside. This army was mostly made up of children who were evacuated  from their homes in the big cities in case of German bomb attacks.

THE OTHER ARMY

In the first big evacuation in 1939 these were evacuated:

12,000 pregnant women.

103,000 teachers and helpers.

827,000 schoolchildren.

524,000 toddlers with their mothers.

+ 7,000 disabled people.

Evacuation meant being sent away from home to somewhere safer.

Some dogs were evacuated too. One advertisement read:

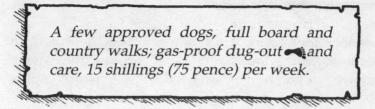

A few approved dogs, full board and country walks; gas-proof dug-out and care, 15 shillings (75 pence) per week.

Sometimes the children wore name-labels on their clothes. When they arrived, people chose which children they wanted to stay with them. It could be a bit like an auction. In other places everything was well-organised in advance.

Sometimes children from well-off families stayed in poor country cottages, and sometimes poor children stayed in large country mansions. If the children came

A *dug-out* was an underground air-raid shelter.

from poor town families, they might never have seen a cow or a sheep before and would have come from miserable conditions at home.

On the other hand, if the families who took them in were well-off, the poor 'evacuees', as they were known, might be the first really poor people these well-off families had ever seen at close quarters. There was a huge gap between the upper and lower classes in those days.

Some of the evacuees had always slept under their parents' bed and they refused to sleep in a proper bed because they weren't used to it.

Many didn't know how to use a toothbrush.

Many of the children's heads were crawling with head lice.

As the Prime Minister said in a letter: '*I never knew such conditions existed, and I feel ashamed of having been so ignorant of my neighbours*'.

Many of the children had a great time in the countryside and loved the comfy cottage beds and playing in the fields. But some of them felt terribly homesick as soon as they arrived. One wrote home on a postcard: *'Dear Mum, I hope you are well. I don't like the man's face much. Perhaps it will look better in the daylight. I like the dog's face best.'*

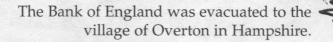

It wasn't just people who were evacuated.

The Bank of England was evacuated to the village of Overton in Hampshire.

The paintings of the National Gallery were moved to a slate quarry in Wales.

ALIENS BEWARE!

Everyone was given a gas mask and expected to carry it with them all the time, in case German planes dropped poison-gas bombs. Gas masks had a snout to breathe through and two eye-holes. When people put them on they looked like aliens from outer space. There were even special gas-proof cots for babies.

SO WHERE'S THE WAR THEN?

So there were all the British - many of them in the armed forces or living with strangers in the countryside, most of them lugging their gas masks around everywhere.

And nothing happened.

Hitler just couldn't make up his mind when to attack. Summer turned to autumn, and autumn to winter. This strange time when nothing happened was called the 'Phoney War'.

That winter of 1939 the British soldiers in France settled down as best they could in odd places such as barns and stables. Many slept on straw. Back in England people stopped carrying their gas masks and the evacuated children drifted back to their homes in the cities.

By the following April the Prime Minister felt able to announce *'Hitler has missed the bus!'* After all, nothing was happening.

Or was it ...?

DAD'S ARMY

WE SHALL FIGHT THEM WITH FORKS – IF WE HAVE TO.

A week later, on 9 April 1940, German armies smashed through Denmark and invaded Norway.

British troops rushed to defend Norway, but were driven off.

WAR ON WHEELS

It was as easy as squashing flies. The German army was the best in Europe. They'd had plenty of practice invading Czechoslovakia and Poland. They were tough soldiers and they moved as quick as lightning.

In fact lightning, or *Blitzkrieg* (meaning 'lightning-war'), was the word they used to describe their tactics. You see, the Germans were the first people to realise that aircraft used with tanks and lorries made war happen much faster than in the past. Everyone else attacked at about the speed of their poor old foot-soldiers, but the Germans barged ahead in tanks, while their special *Stuka* dive-bombers swooped down on the enemy from above. It worked only too well.

FRANCE IN A GLANCE

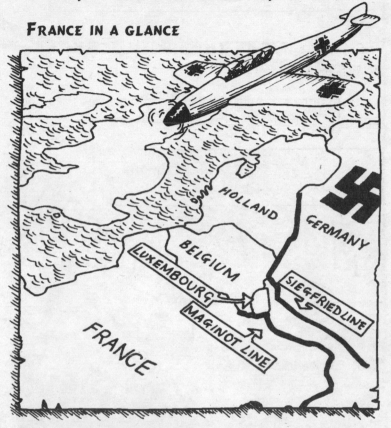

Having gobbled up Norway and Denmark, it was time for the Germans to take a bite at France. The French had built a massive great defence system, called the 'Maginot Line', along their border with Germany, but the Germans simply drove round it, attacking through Belgium on 10 May 1940. Their Blitzkrieg tactics were just as successful against the French and the British as they were against everyone else...

Their aeroplanes towed gliders full of paratroopers to drop behind enemy lines.

Their screeching Stukas dive-bombed helpless foot-soldiers. Stukas were terrifying. They had special sirens which made a screaming noise as they attacked.

They dropped dummy paratroopers to frighten the enemy into thinking there were more of them than there really were.

Their tanks drove in huge herds which crushed all opposition.

In next to no time half of France was occupied by the Germans, and the other half, to be known as 'Vichy France', was ruled by a government which was friendly towards Germany. The French and the British armies were forced back to the English Channel. It looked as if they would have no choice except to drown in the sea or surrender.

But Britain had a secret weapon ...

WINNIE THE POOH!

Winston Churchill, or 'Winnie' for short, loved smoking big, fat, smelly cigars and drank whisky all day. He liked a fight.

After the invasion of Norway, Neville Chamberlain resigned as Prime Minister. He had cancer but also people blamed him for not standing up to the Nazis when the Nazis invaded Czechoslovakia. Winnie took over. He was just what Britain needed.

One thing Winston Churchill would never do was surrender.

RETREAT!

Back in Europe, in June 1940, the British and French armies retreated into a narrow strip of land around the French port of Dunkirk. All the ships available in Britain were sent across the British Channel to carry the troops back to England. There were big warships, cross-channel ferries, even paddle-steamers.

But the big ships couldn't get in close enough to shore for the soldiers to wade out to them. Inspired by Winnie, the call went out for smaller boats to sail across. Soon the Channel was dotted with a vast number of small boats, like a mad yachting regatta.

In a blazing hell of dive-bombers and gun-fire the British ships saved nearly 340,000 men - most of the British army and more than a hundred thousand French soldiers.

It was an amazing escape, but on the other hand the British had suffered sixty-eight thousand casualties.

Once back in England the British soldiers were exhausted but safe. As one said: *'I've had no sleep for a week. I could sleep on a clothes line.'* They were greeted with sandwiches and cups of tea. And their escape had been so amazing and lucky that they were treated more like conquering heroes than a defeated army.

Just one thing was wrong ...

They had left behind 90,000 rifles, 64,000 vehicles, 50,800 tonnes of amunition and stores, as well as many guns. It was only a matter of time before the Germans would try to invade Britain, and Britain had very few weapons left to fight them off.

BELL-RINGING GERMAN GLIDER-PILOT WITH PARACHUTE NEEDED TO REPLACE MISSING SIGNPOSTS

Hardly anyone thought of making peace with the Germans, in spite of Dunkirk. They were encouraged by Winnie, who made a famous speech saying that this was their 'finest hour'. In fact the British felt surprisingly good.

Already many preparations had been made in case of a German invasion, and now everybody worked harder than ever.

All signposts were taken down so that the enemy army would get lost - this probably caused more problems for the British than it would have done for the Germans.

38

Pillboxes were built where it would be easiest to hold up an advancing army, for instance beside bridges. Pillboxes were strong concrete or brick shelters built to protect guns from enemy fire.

> WHAT DO YOU THINK OF THE NEW HOUSE, GIRLS?

> MOO.

Large fields were planted with poles and wire to stop gliders landing.

> I HOPE THEY DON'T GROW!

> WOOF

Railway station signs were taken down. You had to ask people where you were.

> EXCUSE ME, IS THIS SHEFFIELD?

> COULD BE.

> BAAA

> SHSSS!

Bell-ringing was forbidden except as a warning that German paratroopers had arrived.

At last - Dad's Army

To help the regular army, in May 1940 the Government had asked for men aged anywhere between seventeen and sixty-five to report to their local police station and join a new 'Home Guard'.

Men rummaged in dusty cupboards and sheds and grabbed what weapons they could, from old shotguns and World War I rifles to the odd garden fork. Then they marched down to the local police station. So many rushed to join that in one village in Kent the policeman thought he was facing a mob of armed rioters rather than a crowd of law-abiding volunteers. By July the Home Guard had grown to a million and a half members.

Pretty well anyone was welcome. The oldest was in his eighties. There was no medical examination to make sure they were fit. All that was asked was that they had 'free movement', whatever that meant. No one had to have any experience of firing a rifle, although many of them had fought in World War I. In fact, in the early days there weren't that many rifles to fire. They were so short of weapons that at one stage some were given pikes  made of an iron tube with a knife blade on the end.

> SEVEN THOUSAND AND THIRTY-ONE, SEVEN THOUSAND AND THIRTY-TWO...

In July the Home Guard was given 500,000 World War I rifles from America. These had been kept in thick sticky oil since 1918 to stop them going rusty. The job of cleaning them was almost enough to make you want to surrender to the Germans. Just cleaning eight thousand took two hundred and fifty women a fortnight's hard work.

COW OR SEA LION?

It's hard to believe that the Home Guard could have stood up to the Germans for long. They were badly-armed and nervous. Several cows were shot in the dark by members of the Home Guard who thought the cows were German paratroopers.

Pikes are a medieval weapon. They are a very long pole with a blade, spike or axe on the end and were very useful against armoured knights on horseback.

41

And the Germans were gathering barges for the invasion. They had their plan all worked out. It was called *Operation Sea Lion.* The day after their invasion was to be called *S Day.* They were going to attack along the south coast of England and hoped to mop up the whole country in a week or two.

There was just one problem - they had to take control of the skies to stop the British bombing their barges when they crossed the Channel ...

BLACK AS A PIECE OF COAL IN A BLACK BAG

LOST BOMBER SEEKS SPECK OF LIGHT FOR HOMEWARD JOURNEY.

The summer of 1940 was fabulous. One lovely, long, hot, sunny day followed another. England looked beautiful, and although there were some German bomber attacks, it was hard to believe they would ever amount to much. Crowds of sightseers came to see the damage, and little children clambered around the bomb-craters looking for bits of bomb, called shrapnel, to keep.

In 1941 one girl found a German airman's glove in a bomb-crater. She took it home to show to her mum. But when she put it on the kitchen table – she found it had a hand inside it!

Everything looked as peaceful as a cat in a hammock, but in the clear blue sky over southern England a deadly battle was about to start. Goering, the head of the German *Luftwaffe* , had persuaded Hitler that he could win control of the air before the main German invasion started. The first big attack was fixed for 13 August, which was called *Adlertag*, or Eagle Day.

The Battle of Britain had begun.

The *Luftwaffe* (meaning 'Air Weapon') was the German air force.

PILOT PROBLEMS

During the Battle of Britain, the British had too few planes and too few pilots to fly them.

Factories churned out new planes as fast as possible, and people gave money to help build them. Through the Spitfire Fund you could 'buy' a bit of a plane - for instance sixpence for a rivet, twenty-two pounds for a small bomb.

Meanwhile the handful of pilots had to keep flying almost round the clock. As the weeks passed and the battle in the air dragged on, the pilots became exhausted. *'You were too tired even to get drunk,'* as one of them said. They often took off with new wounds quickly bandaged. One young pilot used to be sick every time on his way to the plane, because, in the words of another young pilot: *'Most of us were pretty scared all the bloody time.'*

Then after a few weeks the German pilots were ordered to bomb British cities. This meant that they had little time left over to damage British airfields and planes on the ground. The British could rebuild and repair their air force between battles in the air.

The Germans had made a big mistake. By September 1940 it was clear that they would not be able to destroy the Royal Air Force. The Battle of Britain was over.

BALLOON BATTLE

Cables from barrage balloons were designed to get tangled up in enemy aircraft. You are an enemy bomber. Can you find your way to safety through the British barrage balloons?

EXPECT THE WORST

The Battle of Britain was over, but the bombing of Britain had only just begun. Many German bombers got past the British planes and dropped their bombs on the cities of Britain. In September the Germans started night bombing raids and this went on for the rest of the *Blitz*, as the German bombing was called.

Before the War it was calculated that the Luftwaffe could drop 700,000 kilograms of bombs per day on London. So the Government had expected the worst and planned for it:

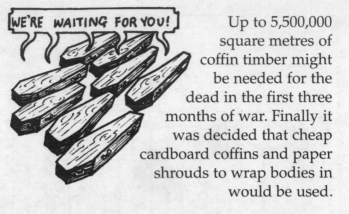

Up to 5,500,000 square metres of coffin timber might be needed for the dead in the first three months of war. Finally it was decided that cheap cardboard coffins and paper shrouds to wrap bodies in would be used.

There might be 4,000,000 mental cases in the first six months, as well as all the other casualties.

As it turned out, things weren't quite that bad. But they were still pretty awful ...

BOMBED TO BLITZ

The first warning of a bombing raid was the wail of the air-raid sirens, followed by the drone of the bombers' engines. Then powerful searchlights pierced the night sky and the anti-aircraft guns started up.

In fact more British civilians than German airmen were killed by anti-aircraft shell-fragments, and one local council said that the vibrations of the guns damaged the toilet bowls in their council houses. But on the other hand, the anti-aircraft guns forced the bombers to fly high, so that they couldn't aim their bombs so well.

In the first stage of the Blitz, up till November, 10,000 people were killed. Which is a lot, but not as many as the Government had expected. The biggest problem turned out to be where to put all the newly-homeless people after their houses were bombed. These bombed-out people were always covered in dirt and dust and were often in their night-clothes. Only a few rest centres were ready for them. Rest centres never had enough places to wash and there was often only bread and margarine to eat.

Fire-bombs or 'incendiaries' caused some of the worst damage. If a fire-bomb fell on a warehouse the result could be spectacular. There were rubber fires producing clouds of dangerous smoke, rum fires (which smelt lovely), and even pepper fires which made your eyes water. During one blaze it was possible to read a newspaper in Shaftesbury Avenue in London by the light of flames five miles away.

> Sometimes the rats would be driven from their nests and thousands of them would run through the streets.

ORDINARY HEROES

Some of the bravest people in the War weren't in the armed forces at all.

 Firemen often fought fires while bombs fell around them.

 Fire watchers, armed only with a stirrup pump and a water bucket, put out many small fires before they could blaze up.

 ARP (stands for Air Raid Precautions) wardens each controlled an area of about five hundred people. Mostly they were part-time.

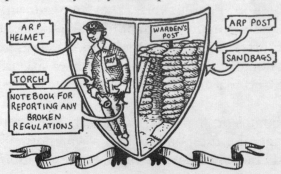

ARP HELMET

ARP POST

WARDEN'S POST

SANDBAGS

TORCH

NOTEBOOK FOR REPORTING ANY BROKEN REGULATIONS

SHELTERING FROM THE BLAST

Most of Britain's major cities were badly bombed, but London got the worst of it. When the air-raid siren sounded, everyone rushed for shelter.

They might take refuge in an 'Anderson Shelter'. In the garden a pit was dug and covered by a curved roof made from fourteen sheets of corrugated steel. Then earth was piled on top. Vegetables were often planted on the roof.

Other people stayed indoors in a 'Morrison Shelter'. This was a large box with a steel roof. It could stand up to the collapse of a two-storey house.

Advice for dog owners: *'When you take him in the shelter, put him on a lead. If you can put a muzzle on him you should do so because he may get hysterical during the raids. Put some cotton-wool in his ears.'*

Designed by Dr David Anderson, production and distribution organised by Home Secretary, Sir John Anderson.

Named after Herbert Morrison, Minister of Home Security.

Eighty London underground stations were used as air-raid shelters at night. Some people would queue all day for a place on the platform for their families. Library services were provided, and a few stations were fitted out with bunk-beds. But underground stations were uncomfortable. They were a breeding ground for lice, and deep under ground, below the level of main sewage drains, there were no toilets because at that depth there were no drains beneath the stations for the toilets to drain into.

YOU'LL JUST HAVE TO WAIT TILL MORNING.

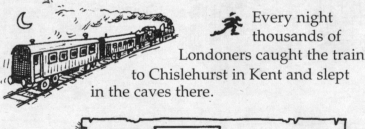

Every night thousands of Londoners caught the train to Chislehurst in Kent and slept in the caves there.

CLEAR OFF, ROVER!

Dogs were forbidden in public air-raid shelters.

There were shelters in the basements of some very strong buildings.

Trench shelters were dug in public squares.

The Germans also had air-raid shelters. Some of the Berlin shelters were huge. The one under Berlin Zoo could sleep ten thousand.

ROOM FOR ONE MORE?

ACHTUNG!

SPOT THE SPY

The animals have taken over the shelter beneath Berlin Zoo. One is a British spy - but which is it?

Answer: The one with the briefcase.

BLACK-OUT!

Every night everyone in Britain suffered from black-out. This didn't mean that they became unconscious; the idea of the black-out was to stop German bombers from seeing the lights of towns and villages. Every light had to be covered up:

Night-trains had their blinds drawn, with only a blue pinpoint of light on the ceiling in each compartment. They were really gloomy.

Black-out curtains were fastened to all windows.

Traffic lights were fitted with hoods on top and black shields showing only a small cross of light at the front for each colour.

Torches had to be covered with two layers of tissue paper.

Train and bus windows were covered against flying glass, with just a small slit to let passengers see the name of the station or bus-stop. The buses were so dark inside that bus conductors had a hard job seeing what money they were given. Many dud coins were handed over.

One good thing came of it all: for the first time in more than a hundred years the stars could be seen shining clearly over London and other big cities.

And one bad thing came of it: the number of road accidents more than doubled. Car headlights were covered. Only a tiny slit was left uncovered to shine light down onto the road.

The Germans had a black-out too. Keen Nazis wore luminous buttons in the shape of the *swastika* .

The *swastika* was the symbol of the Nazis. It's based on an ancient Hindu sign meaning 'well-being'.

All Clear!

Germany had lost the Battle of Britain by September 1940, but the Blitz went on until May 1941, even though it was clear that the Germans had lost their chance to invade England.

Then in June 1941 the Germans invaded Russia instead. For the British, the worst was over - for the time being.

The Blitz had been a terrible experience. Many people saw their loved ones die and their homes destroyed. But despite their suffering, the British people had shown themselves to be very brave and to be as tough as old leather.

Britain had survived to fight on.

WHAT'S A BANANA?

AND THE CUPBOARD WAS BARE ...

WOLF PACKS

Britain, in case you haven't noticed, is an island. Everything Britain needs from outside has to come by ship or aeroplane. Hitler set out to sink Britain's ships and to starve her of vital supplies such as petrol, metal and food.

In fact, on the very day war was declared, a German submarine sank the British liner, Athenia, bound for Canada. Soon British ships were being sunk in their hundreds and many British sailors died.

The Battle of the Atlantic, the longest battle of World War II, had started.

The biggest threat to British ships was German submarines, *Untersee Boote* - or U-Boats as they were called in English. The U-Boats hunted the stormy seas of the North Atlantic in groups known as 'wolf packs', seeking to cut Britain's vital supplies of food, metals and other raw materials from North America.

SHEEP-DOGS

At the start of the War Britain had the largest fleet of merchant ships in the world, but that wouldn't last long once the U-Boats got their teeth into them. Soon the merchant ships were organised into convoys for the voyage from America. Each convoy was protected by warships of the Royal Navy.

Convoys might be over a hundred ships long, stretching for miles and miles across the Ocean. The warships would sail in front and behind and along the sides, like sheep-dogs working a flock of sheep.

AND SITTING DUCKS

The warships did their best to keep the U-Boats at bay, but once U-Boats were in among the ships of a British convoy they could do a lot of damage.

One of the most unpleasant jobs of the War was to be a merchant sailor in the North Atlantic, chugging along in a large unarmed ship and knowing that U-Boats were lurking in the dark waters below. Huge numbers of British ships were sunk and their sailors drowned or tossed in life-rafts in the icy sea.

But just enough supplies got through to keep Britain going ...

GROW YOUR OWN!

Due to the loss of so many supply-ships, if the British weren't very careful they might be starved into surrendering. So food was as important for the war effort as guns and bullets. The slogan of the day was '*Dig for Victory*!'.

 Vegetable patches were grown in public parks and private front gardens. Allotments spread across the land.

 Farmers grew more crops on their land with the help of extra workers.

 Many households kept hens or a pig. There were 'pig clubs' for those who wanted part share of a pig.

NO, YOU CAN'T HAVE ANY MORE!

There was a better chance of eating a badger than a banana. Food and drink which could not be grown in Britain, such as oranges, tea and bananas, was soon in very short supply. Some people never saw a banana until the War was over.

The Government started a system of rationing, which guaranteed a small but equal quantity of some basic foods for everybody. In fact, poor people ate better in the War than they had before it started. In general people ate fewer meat and dairy products, and there were fewer heart attacks.

At the start, butter, sugar and bacon were rationed. Rations per person per week were:

Butter 113 grams
Sugar 793 grams
Bacon 113 grams

Other foods were rationed later. Everyone had a ration book. They could save up 'points' and spend them all in one go if they wanted to.

The Germans had rationing too, although until towards the end of the War they were better fed than the British. One thing they had enough of was bread. You could often see people in Berlin parks trying to throw away stale bread without being noticed.

Powdered egg - yum!

Most food was dull, and some of it was downright revolting. A lot of eggs were dried and powdered to stop them going bad. It's hard to meet anyone who lived during that time who has a kind word for powdered egg, even though the Government tried to convince them that it was delicious.

The Government suggested lots of different recipes:

```
Carrot marmalade, to help you see in
the dark during the black-out.
Rosehip syrup - good for vitamin C.
Cakes made with powdered egg.
```

Roast eagle

Lots of people ate out on cheap food sold in canteens and elsewhere. This was mainly because so many women were working full-time for the war effort that they didn't have time to cook for their families in the traditional way. The handful of posh restaurants had to use their imagination to produce interesting food. A hotel in Scotland offered gulls' eggs, rooks, and once, 'Roast Eagle and Two Veg'.

WOULD YOU CARE FOR A TALON?

MAKE DO AND MEND

It wasn't just food that was rationed. Rationing was brought in for clothes in 1941, and as the War went on, people's clothes got shabbier and shabbier as they became worn out.

HERS

JEWELLERY FROM BOTTLE TOPS.

MASCARA MADE FROM BURNT CORK.

Tip for making silk stockings last longer - wash in methylated spirits and store in an air-tight jar.

STOCKINGS WERE SO RARE THAT SOME WOMEN PUT TEA OR GRAVY BROWNING ON THEIR BARE LEGS AND PAINTED 'SEAMS' ON THEM.

'UTILITY' DRESS. UTILITY GOODS WERE WELL-DESIGNED.

ANY OLD BITS OF TORN PARACHUTE SILK WERE USED FOR UNDERWEAR AND OTHER LUXURY ITEMS.

Recipe for Soap-Free Bath
Stew pine needles.
Pour the liquid into
your bath.
You may smell like a pine forest,
but you'll be nice and clean!

His

TO SAVE CLOTH, LAWS LIMITED THE STYLE OF MEN'S CLOTHES.

ONLY SINGLE-BREASTED JACKETS WERE ALLOWED.

A LAW LIMITED THE NUMBER OF POCKETS ON MEN'S JACKETS.

A LAW LIMITED THE LENGTH OF MEN'S SHIRT-TAILS.

TURN-UPS ON MEN'S TROUSERS WERE ILLEGAL.

SOCKS WERE DARNED AGAIN AND AGAIN.

FUEL GRUEL

Without fuel, a tank or a battleship is little more than a useless lump of metal. Fuel was food and drink to the armed forces, and as such it was as important to the war effort as food itself. It was vital not to waste precious petrol on non-military uses. Government posters asked: *'Is your journey really necessary?'*. To start with, petrol rations were enough to allow two hundred miles' travel per month for every car, but later all private motoring was banned.

People such as doctors who needed their cars for work could combine business with pleasure. For instance, a doctor could go to the shops while out visiting one of his or her patients.

BLACK MARKET

If you had the money, you could nearly always get what you wanted - despite rationing. Crooks like me, known as 'spivs', sold scarce goods on the illegal 'black market'. The goods we sold on the black market were often either stolen from somewhere or had been sold illegally by a farmer or shopkeeper outside the rationing system. Prices on the black market were much higher than elsewhere.

The police tried hard to stop the black market. For instance petrol might be dyed red. If they found traces of the dye in your engine, you could be fined. But they never managed to stamp out the black market.

HA! THIS SHOULD HELP.

WASTE NOT WANT NOT

There was a use for everything. If the Government could have found a use for old toilet paper it would have done so. This would have been difficult because there wasn't any toilet paper at that time - people used cut squares of newspaper.

ONE THOUSAND AND ONE, ONE THOUSAND AND TWO...

Everything that could be recycled was recycled:

Paper was useful for cases for shells and for recycling.

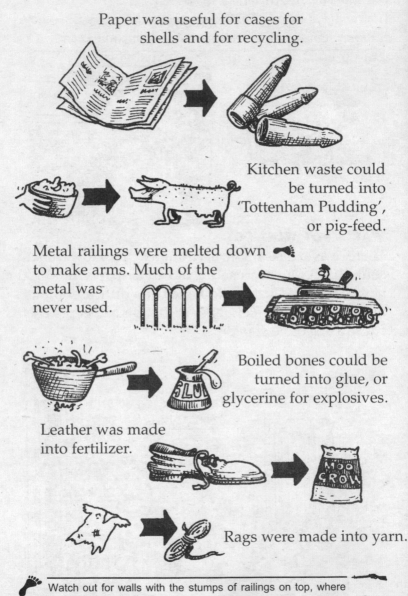

Kitchen waste could be turned into 'Tottenham Pudding', or pig-feed.

Metal railings were melted down to make arms. Much of the metal was never used.

Boiled bones could be turned into glue, or glycerine for explosives.

Leather was made into fertilizer.

Rags were made into yarn.

Watch out for walls with the stumps of railings on top, where they were sawn off.

USEFUL TIPS No 1 - IN THE KITCHEN

Clean your woodwork with tea-dregs.
If you have some fresh eggs, crush the egg shells to
make a scouring powder.
Cut up your old mac to make the baby's bib.

USEFUL TIPS No 2 - AT SCHOOL

Write with thin, brittle pencils or a
scratchy dip-in pen. Use your pencil
down to the last two centimetres.

Use every bit of your exercise
book, leave no margins and
write all over the front and
back covers.

BLIMMIN WIMMIN

WHAT GREAT-GRANDMA DID IN THE WAR.

Millions of women took on jobs normally done by men. By the end of the War all fit women between eighteen and fifty-one had to work if they were asked to.

A LIST OF LIVELY LADIES

WOMEN WARRIORS

Women flocked to join the armed services. By the end of the War there were half a million in uniform. They did vital support work such as repairing aircraft and ships.

They were known by their initials:

WRNS, or *Wrens*, the Women's Royal Naval Service.
WAAFS, Women's Auxiliary Air Force.
ATS, Auxiliary Territorial Service.

FEMALE FARMERS

Most male farm labourers joined the army, so there weren't enough workers left on the farms. Food was desperately needed because of the Battle of the Atlantic. Enter the Women's Land Army.

Land girls had to work wherever they were sent, and they only got seven days' leave per year to go home. The work was often very tiring, especially if they came from a soft life in the city, but most of them were up to any challenge. Here are some typical Land Army jobs:

LAND GIRL

TREE FELLING

RAT CATCHING

MILKING

POTATO PICKING

HARVESTING

FACTORY FODDER

The munitions factories, which churned out tanks, guns and planes to replace those destroyed by the enemy, were mainly worked by women. Special nurseries were laid on so that women with children could work if a factory was near their home.

Clippies
During the War, most bus-conductors were female.

 ### Civil Defence
Brave young women operated the floodlights to pick out enemy bombers. They also fired the anti-aircraft guns, although they weren't really meant to.

WVS
The Women's Voluntary Service helped out all over the place. They helped with evacuation, took food to bombed-out houses and greeted the survivors of Dunkirk.

✠ FINICKY FRAULEINS ✠

While British women were expected to help with the war effort, before the War the Nazis discouraged German women from working. As already noted, German women were expected to stay at home and breed new members of the Master Race. It wasn't important whether they married or not - so long as they had children.

Real advertisement in a German newspaper:

> Two vital, lusty, race-conscious Brünhildes desirous of serving their fatherland in the form most ennobling women, would like to make the acquaintance of two similarly-inclined Siegfrieds. Marriage not of essential importance.

However, once the War started, the Nazis realised that they needed more women to work in the factories because so many German men were in the army. But now they had the problem of convincing the women that they should work outside the home after all.

They weren't very successful.

And when the hours of factory work were lengthened, there was a big rise in the number of German women then in work who stayed at home sick.

FEATHERED FRIEND

This bird has joined the Royal Navy due to a misunderstanding. What kind of bird is it?

1. A Golden Eagle
2. A Buzzard
3. A Wren

Answer 1. A Wren of course - this meant WRNS or Women's Royal Naval Service.

72

WORKERS' PLAYTIME

HEE HEE AND HAW HAW.

WILLING WORKERS - AND NOT SO WILLING

The problem with war is that the other side keeps destroying all your tanks, ships and other gear. It's a hard job to keep up, let alone increase the amount of weapons for your forces to use. So factories are as important as armies - which is why the other side tries to bomb them, of course. Towards the end of the War there were five million people doing war work (which included working on the land), many of them women, all busy as ants in an antheap.

Thousands of small businesses turned their hands to producing war material. For instance some furniture makers made parts for an all-wood plane, the 'Wooden Wonder', otherwise known as the De Havilland Mosquito.

And hundreds of brand-new factories were built, some of them underground to avoid the bombs. Near Bath, 279,000 square metres of old stone-quarry became an underground aircraft factory.

Without fuel all the tanks and ships made in the factories would be useless, and without fuel the factories would have been useless as well. Fortunately, at the time of the Second World War many factories ran on coal, and Britain had enough coal for all its needs; the only problem was digging it out. This is why mining became a 'reserved occupation', meaning that miners weren't allowed to join the armed forces. Lots of conscientious objectors worked in the mines, and, towards the end of the War, many men who wanted to join the army had to go and work in the mines instead. It was that important.

As for the unwilling workers: prisoners of war also helped with the war effort. Apart from thousands of Italians, there were 400,000 German prisoners in Britain by the end of the War, 90,000 of them working on the land. Many chose to stay on after the War was over. One such, Bert Trautmann, became famous as the goalkeeper for Manchester City.

Things were different in Germany, where millions of workers from the conquered lands in Poland, Czechoslovakia and Russia were treated like slaves. They worked as little as they could get away with and would 'put a spanner in the works' if possible. But if they were caught, punishments for undermining the Nazi war effort were horrific, including beating and starvation.

WHAT! NO TELLY?

In a war, morale is very important. What this means is that if people are happy and believe they can win, they will work and fight much harder than if they are depressed and think they are going to lose.

So it was important to keep the workers happy. There was no television during the War and everyone listened to the wireless. Wireless was the best way to cheer them up.

 Music While You Work was pumped into countless factories over their loud-speaker systems.

 ITMA (*It's That Man Again*) was a very popular radio and television comedy.

 Workers' Playtime was a lunchtime programme that came on three times a week in factory canteens, and was recorded in canteens around the country.

E-VERY N-IGHT S-OMETHING A-WFUL

As well as radio programmes, the Government organised live shows. The original idea behind ENSA, the Entertainments National Service Association, was to cheer up the troops by putting on special travelling shows. There were ENSA performers with the army when it escaped from the Germans at Dunkirk. Later there were ENSA shows in factories as well. They performed in the canteens during lunch-breaks.

GOOSE-STEPS AND PROPER GANDERS

In a war, governments try to persuade their people that they are fighting for the right side and that their side is winning - even if it isn't. They make sure lots of encouraging news stories appear in the papers and on the television and radio. They also give out pamphlets and posters. All this stuff is called 'propaganda'.

British and American propaganda told people that the British side were kind and democratic, and that the Nazis were evil maniacs who shouted all the time and goose-stepped 🐾 around in jack-boots, trying to conquer the world - which was all true up to a point.

German propaganda told its people that their enemies were trying to destroy Europe and that the Germans, led by the Nazis, were trying to defend it - which wasn't really true at all.

HAW HAW

War-time governments mostly use propaganda to gee-up their own people, but they also use it to make the enemy population feel bad. The Nazis used to beam a

---

The *goose-step* is a style of marching where the leg is raised very high and straight in front.

radio programme into Britain, telling us how badly we were doing in the War.

They found an Irish Nazi called William Joyce who was willing to be their announcer. He was nick-named 'Lord Haw Haw' by the British press because he tried to talk with an upper-class English accent. (Try laughing in an upper-class way - 'haw, haw, haw'.) Sometimes Lord Haw Haw's propaganda was strangely accurate, such as when he reported the exact time that the church clock had stopped in one English village. At other times it sounded like the make-believe of a maniac, such as when he said that a British battleship had been 'hit in the kettles'.

Lord Haw Haw kept working till the end of the War. He made his last broadcast blind drunk in the ruins of Berlin, just before Germany surrendered. After the War he was tried for high treason in London and executed.

RESIST IF YOU DARE!

LIFE ON THE OTHER SIDE.

LET ME OUT!

Europeans didn't want to be ruled by the Germans and didn't like the Nazis lording it over them. They wanted to be able to speak and read freely and to come and go as they pleased.

Fat hope! The Nazis ruled Europe with an iron hand. If one of their soldiers was killed, they were likely to shoot several innocent citizens in cold blood as a *reprisal*.
Sometimes hundreds of innocent people were rounded-up and shot. Most people kept their heads down and got on with their lives as best they could. They showed their anger at the Germans by walking out of restaurants if a German entered and other such unfriendly acts.

Most people but not all. Some brave souls fought back. They were known as the 'Resistance'.

Secrecy was vital. The Resistance was organised in 'networks'. Each network stayed as separate as possible from other networks so that if one was betrayed the others would not be affected.

THE WORK OF A RESISTANCE AGENT
There was plenty of work for the Resistance to do:

Help Jews escape.

Help prisoners of war escape.

Blow up railway lines.

Blow up factories.

Resistance fighters were very brave. They risked betrayal at any time. There were always plenty of people who hated having a Resistance member living in their town or village. Such people feared German reprisal shootings more than they wanted freedom from German rule.

If a Resistance agent or a secret agent from Britain was caught, they could expect no mercy. The SS would torture their victims in order to get them to give away information about other agents or Resistance fighters.

The torture and questioning might go on for weeks. Then when it was over the prisoner would probably be shot or sent away to *Nacht und Nebel,* or 'night and fog' in English. This meant being sent off to a German concentration camp and almost certain death.

SWING STORY

There was resistance in Germany too. One small piece of resistance was the 'Swing Youth Movement' which was partly about non-Nazi fashion and partly about non-Nazi music. The Nazis hated the Swing Youth Movement because Swing youths liked jazz, which had been invented by black Americans.

The Swing boys wore English-style clothes with a rolled-up umbrella, and the girls wore lots of un-Nazi make-up. The typical Swing youth whistled English hit tunes all the time. When they met each other they gave the Nazi straight-arm salute, but instead of saying 'heil Hitler', they said 'heil Benny' after the American dance band leader, Benny Goodman.

It couldn't last. They were soon rounded-up and sent to concentration camps to be punished.

Rebel Armies

In France, Greece and Yugoslavia secret resistance armies sprang up. They set up camps in the wild hills and forests, ready to attack the Germans.

The French resistance army was called the *Maquis*, from the French word for the scrubby landscape where they hid. They were loyal to the 'Free French' government whose leader, General De Gaulle, was based in London. The *Maquis* was mainly made up of young men who

De Gaulle

fled into the mountains in Southern France to avoid being shipped off to work in German factories. They slept in caves or built themselves log cabins and sprang surprise raids on German troops. In the Battle of Vercors 3,500 *Maquisards* fought unsuccessfully against 20,000 Germans. Around seven hundred *Maquisards* died.

Collaborate if you don't dare!

The Germans ruled through their army and the *SS*, but they also made use of local police forces and local Nazi sympathizers. People who helped the Germans were known as 'collaborators'. Every occupied country had lots of them. In several countries it was the local police who rounded-up Jews to be sent to German concentration camps.

There were many collaborators in France. Three

thousand Frenchmen joined SS army divisions, and there were plenty of political parties which collaborated as well. Worst of all were the *Milice Francais*. They were a force of about ninety thousand men who wore black berets. They loved to crush the Resistance and to bully the Jews in their areas.

The SS and the Milice were desperate to stamp out all opposition to their rule. They knew that many people were working secretly to overthrow them ...

SPIES

CAN YOU KEEP A SECRET?

SOE WHAT?

'Special Operations Executive' agents were volunteers who were dropped behind enemy lines to work with the local Resistance to cause as much trouble to the enemy as possible.

You have to be a very brave person to be dropped on to an unknown field at night in an enemy country with nothing but an old suitcase of spare clothes and a false name.

During the War around one and a half thousand agents were dropped into France alone. If they were caught they were treated like spies, because they did not wear uniforms like proper soldiers. If captured, soldiers in uniform were made prisoners of war, but agents and spies, dressed in civilian clothes, were usually tortured and shot.

JUST SOE STORY

SOE agent, South African George Dessing, was dropped by parachute - right into the middle of an SS training camp! After giving Nazi salutes to the guards, he casually walked out without being stopped.

Later the Germans used another agent called Leonard Andringa, whom they had caught and terrified into helping them, to lure Dessing to a meeting in a café. But Dessing sensed that something was wrong. Again he casually walked out - right past Andringa's German guard.

Realising that he was useless now that the Germans knew who he was, Dessing decided to escape. It took him a year to cross occupied Europe to neutral Switzerland.

CLASSIFIED CLASSROOM

Before they set off, the SOE agents had special training.

How to hide secret messages in a rolled up cigarette - and smoke it if in trouble.

How to pick locks, blow up safes and general burglary.

Methods of escape.

How to blow up bridges, railways and other targets.

How to work a pocket radio transmitter.

Never to greet friends in the street.

And lots more ...

ANY MORE IDEAS ON ESCAPE METHODS?

RECIPE FOR A GOOD AGENT

Agents needed to know:

> How to behave in a foreign country. (One woman looked right when she wanted to cross the road, as if she were still in Britain where traffic drives on the left. It was enough to get her arrested.)

> How to speak the language fluently.

Agents needed the right kind of personality:

> They had to be good at acting.

> If they were too daring they wouldn't last long enough.

> If they were too careful they would stay alive but they wouldn't get anything done. SOE work was nearly always dangerous.

> They had to be able to live in a constant state of fear.

There were quite a lot of female agents. The theory was that they were less likely to be stopped by the police, because men who were not fighting or working might be stopped and questioned. Also women were thought to be better able to charm their way out of trouble.

THE DROP

Sometimes agents were landed by boat on a lonely moonlit shore. More often they were taken to their destination by 'Lysander'.

The Lysander was a very special plane which was designed to drop agents and supplies into enemy territory. So as to be able to fly more than a thousand kilometres without refuelling, it had no guns or bombs or any extra weight. It could land in a field less than thirty-two metres long and take off again within just four minutes.

On the approach to their drop-point the pilots would swoop down to as low as 152 metres. Enemy searchlights were designed to aim high in the sky and they couldn't pick out low-flying planes.

All the pilot had to aim for might be a torch flashing in some bushes or a few small lights to mark out a landing field. Often they didn't even land, and they dropped their load, which might be an agent or supplies for the Resistance, by parachute.

Then the pilot flew back to England, but the poor old agent was alone in enemy territory - in the dark.

Agents were usually met by the local Resistance. But if things went wrong, they were on their own.

SIS

SOE agents weren't spies. Spies operated completely secretly and almost nobody knew who they were. One spy with access to reliable information, for instance on enemy troop movements, could be more valuable than a whole army of soldiers. So both sides lived in fear that enemy spies would give away their most secret decisions. British spies worked for the SIS, or Secret Intelligence Service (nowadays called MI6) which also tried to catch German spies.

Often the most useful information could be picked up by spies reading the newspapers or listening to conversations in the street. British government propaganda told people to be careful who they talked to in case a spy overheard them. Propaganda posters used slogans such as, *'careless talk costs lives'*, *'keep Mum - she's not so dumb'*.

SECRET CODES

Spies were useful, but code-breaking was even more useful. Most orders from the German Government to German troops and ships were sent by radio. It was easy to pick up the radio messages on radio masts in England. The problem was that they had all been turned into secret code on a machine like a typewriter, called *Enigma*.

1. Messages were scrambled up on an Enigma Machine.

SPUNGLE POODLE GLOT XXYW...

2. The scrambled messages were sent by radio.

3. The messages were fed into another Enigma Machine at the other end which had the same settings as the sending machine.

Unfortunately there were millions of different possible settings and the code was incredibly difficult to crack. But whoever cracked it would know what the Germans were planning, and where and when.

Fortunately the Poles had already worked out how Enigma worked and made a copy of the German machine.

Using the Polish information, the British set out to crack Enigma messages on a daily basis. They set up ULTRA (for Ultra-Secret), a special top-secret code-cracking operation, at Bletchley in Buckinghamshire. At its peak, more than ten thousand people worked there, including several brilliant mathematicians. The Germans never found out that ULTRA could read their secret Enigma messages.

I Spy

A German spy is listening to people talking in a café. He's not sure what all their words mean. Suppose you were a traitor - would you be able to help him?

1. **A doodle-bug is ...**
   a. A scribbled drawing
   b. A flying bomb
   c. An insect which sucks blood slowly

2. **Lee Enfield is ...**
   a. A famous cricketer
   b. An ace fighter-pilot
   c. A rifle

3. **An evacuee is ...**
   a. The result of a stomach complaint
   b. Someone who is moved away from their home to a less dangerous area
   c. A thermos flask

Answers
1 - b. 2 - c. 3 - b.

LET'S ALL JOIN IN

WELL IT IS A WORLD WAR!

HORSE-MEAT IN WINTER

FRIENDS NO.1

The Nazis believed that Russian Communism was part of a Jewish plot to weaken Germany and stop the Nazi plan for a German empire. So when Hitler signed an agreement with the powerful Russian leader, Joseph Stalin ☜ , in 1939, the German people were amazed - as were the Russians.

BUT NOT FOR LONG

By summer 1940 Hitler had started to worry that the Russians might decide to attack Germany from the east. Also the Battle of Britain was going badly. So he stopped his plans for invading Britain and attacked Russia in June 1941.

Stalin is Russian for 'steel'. His real name was *Iosif Vissarionovich Dzhugashvili*. No wonder he changed it!

FRIENDS NO.2

Now that Russia was fighting Germany, Britain and Russia became allies. The British papers called Joseph Stalin, the Russian leader, 'Uncle Joe', as if he were a kind, jolly uncle, although really Stalin was a brutal dictator.

THAT'LL TEACH YOU!

The German armies struck deep into Russian territory. The Russian army was weak: Stalin had shot around half his own generals out of fear that they would rebel against him.

STAINLESS STEEL TEETH

Stalin started to reorganise the Russian army. He chose new, younger generals. One of them had stainless steel false teeth, because his real teeth had been kicked out by Stalin's police.

GENERAL WINTER

The Germans were defeated by the Russian weather as much as by the Russian army. Heavy showers of rain began to fall after they had struck deep into Russian territory. The rain turned the sandy roads to mud. The German lorries and even their tanks got stuck in it. They had to wait again and again for the mud to dry. Their advance slowed to a crawl.

They reached within 15 km of Moscow, but when *General Winter*, as the Russians called it, started in December the Germans were really in trouble. Not only did they lack winter clothing, but their supplies ran short ...

Wine for the officers froze and broke the bottles.

Butter was so cold it had to be sawn off the block.

Meat had to be hacked from frozen horses using axes.

LENINGRAD

The greatest siege of the War took place in Russia. Leningrad, or St Petersburg as it's known today, was the second largest city in the country. Before it was freed in January 1944 it was besieged by the Germans for 890 days. One and a half million people died.

RATS IN SUMMER

Meanwhile, in an attempt to divide the Germans and take the heat off the Russians, the British and Allied armies were fighting in Greece and North Africa.

The Allies beat the Italians in North Africa, but when they advanced into Greece they were defeated by the Germans and had to retreat back to Africa again.

In the battles that followed two brilliant generals faced each other.

FIELD MARSHAL ROMMEL
(The Desert Fox)

FIELD MARSHAL
MONTGOMERY

Rommel took over command of the German army in North Africa in February 1941. He soon won a series of brilliant victories over the British and their allies. But then, led by Montgomery and with help from their allies, the British, or 'Desert Rats' as those in North Africa were known, started to win.

By May 1943 the British and recently-arrived Americans had driven Rommel's troops from Africa and they had started on the long, slow fight up Italy.

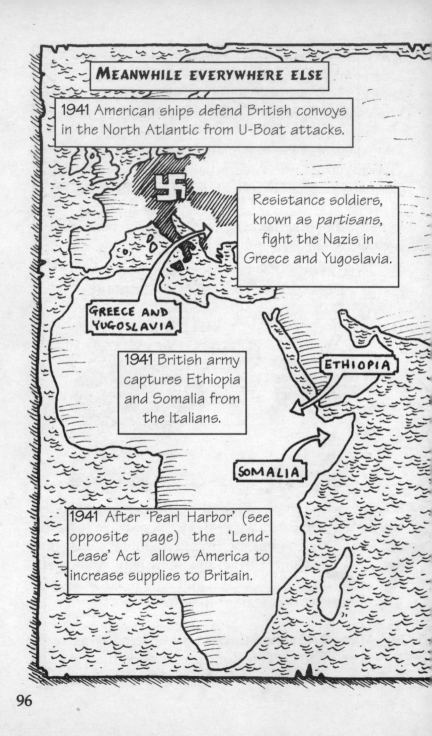

MEANWHILE EVERYWHERE ELSE

1941 American ships defend British convoys in the North Atlantic from U-Boat attacks.

Resistance soldiers, known as *partisans*, fight the Nazis in Greece and Yugoslavia.

GREECE AND YUGOSLAVIA

1941 British army captures Ethiopia and Somalia from the Italians.

ETHIOPIA

SOMALIA

1941 After 'Pearl Harbor' (see opposite page) the 'Lend-Lease' Act allows America to increase supplies to Britain.

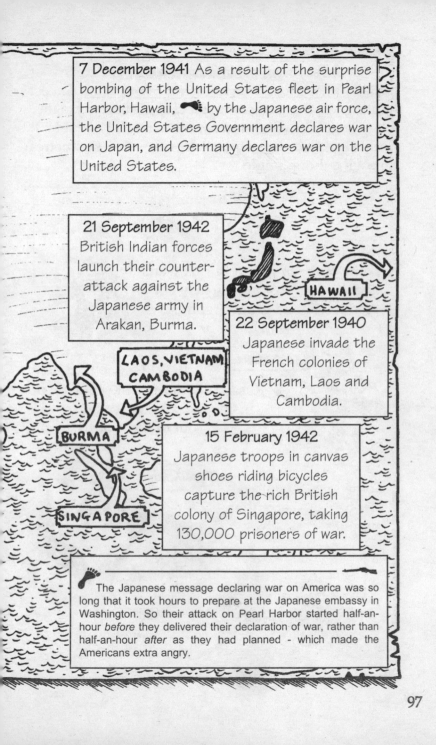

7 December 1941 As a result of the surprise bombing of the United States fleet in Pearl Harbor, Hawaii, 👣🔫 by the Japanese air force, the United States Government declares war on Japan, and Germany declares war on the United States.

21 September 1942 British Indian forces launch their counter-attack against the Japanese army in Arakan, Burma.

HAWAII

LAOS, VIETNAM CAMBODIA

22 September 1940 Japanese invade the French colonies of Vietnam, Laos and Cambodia.

BURMA

SINGAPORE

15 February 1942 Japanese troops in canvas shoes riding bicycles capture the rich British colony of Singapore, taking 130,000 prisoners of war.

The Japanese message declaring war on America was so long that it took hours to prepare at the Japanese embassy in Washington. So their attack on Pearl Harbor started half-an-hour *before* they delivered their declaration of war, rather than half-an-hour *after* as they had planned - which made the Americans extra angry.

JUNGLE FEVER

The Japanese tried to capture the British colony of India by attacking through Burma. Some of the fiercest fighting of the War took place in eastern jungles, where fighting conditions were incredibly tough. It could take five days to travel just twelve kilometres through a thorn jungle.

Fleas were a major problem in Burma.

Some of the troops in Burma weren't allowed to shave in case they cut themselves and caught typhus.

In Sri Lanka the deadly Russell's Viper used to snuggle up inside the soldiers' capes to keep out of the monsoon rain.

Sometimes they used elephants to carry their supplies.

 Mosquitoes were a problem almost everywhere. Their bites itched and they could cause malaria.

NAZIS AND NATIONALISTS

Not everyone in the British Empire and other countries outside Europe wanted to help the British. Some who were struggling for independence backed the Nazis.

CHANDRA BOSE

Large parts of India had been ruled by the British for over a hundred years. Most educated Indians wanted the British to leave, but did not want to use force to drive them out. However some Indians, like Subhas Chandra Bose, wanted to side with Germany and Japan. Bose became commander of the 'Indian National Army', supported by the Japanese.

RASCHID ALI

Iraq was controlled by the British at the start of the war. Raschid Ali was an Iraqi Prime Minister who backed an Arab rebellion against the British.

Luckily for the British however, the Nazis were so nasty that they managed to make enemies out of most people who might otherwise have been their friends.

Soldier's Choice

Are you a northerner or a southerner?

You are colonel of a crack British paratroop regiment. Your regiment is trained to fight in some of the toughest countries in the world.

You have a choice between two missions. Which do you choose?

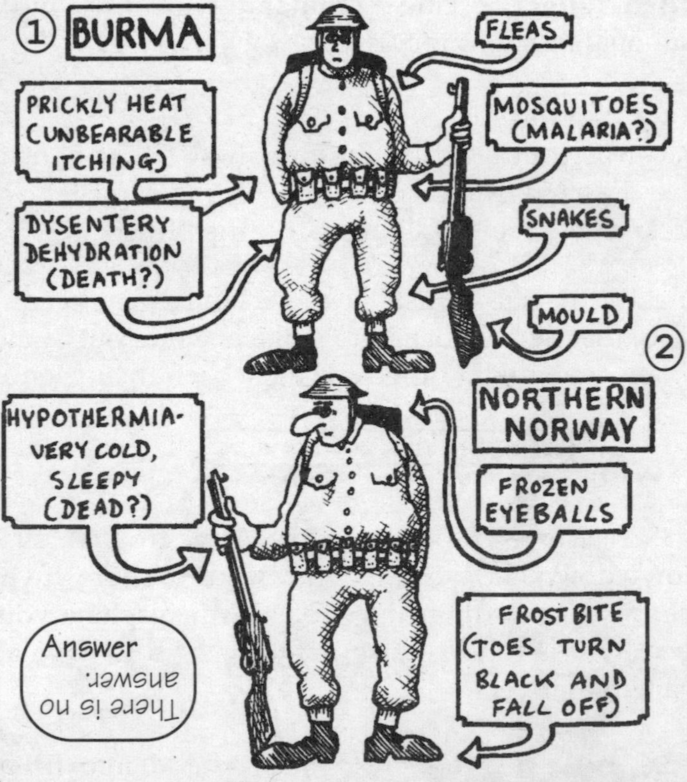

① **BURMA**

FLEAS

PRICKLY HEAT (UNBEARABLE ITCHING)

MOSQUITOES (MALARIA?)

DYSENTERY DEHYDRATION (DEATH?)

SNAKES

MOULD

②

HYPOTHERMIA- VERY COLD, SLEEPY (DEAD?)

NORTHERN NORWAY

FROZEN EYEBALLS

FROSTBITE (TOES TURN BLACK AND FALL OFF)

Answer

There is no answer.

100

BATTLESHIP BRITAIN

GETTING READY FOR THE OFF

BODY BUILDING

Immediately after their retreat from Dunkirk the British started on plans to invade Nazi-occupied Europe - just as soon as they and their allies were strong enough. By 1942 the Russians were asking them to hurry up and get on with it. An Allied invasion in the west would draw German forces away from their war with the Russians in the east.

Landing an army on an enemy shore is just about the hardest thing to do in wartime. Your troops will be mown down like skittles as they wade to shore. If your enemy army is the ruthless Nazi war machine you'll need a massive great army of your own to have any chance of success.

From 1941, men and machines poured into Britain from America and elsewhere. Before long Britain was bristling with guns like the quills on a porcupine, and there were enough men hidden in training camps in southern England to crush the German army just by sitting on it - if they could only get ashore in Europe.

WHERE YOU FROM THEN?

By spring 1944, 1,421,000 foreign troops had gathered in Britain. They came from all over the world.

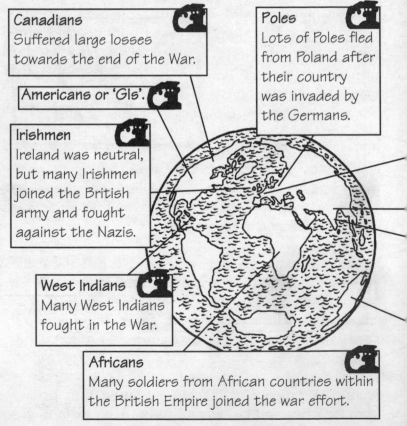

Canadians
Suffered large losses towards the end of the War.

Poles
Lots of Poles fled from Poland after their country was invaded by the Germans.

Americans or 'GIs'.

Irishmen
Ireland was neutral, but many Irishmen joined the British army and fought against the Nazis.

West Indians
Many West Indians fought in the War.

Africans
Many soldiers from African countries within the British Empire joined the war effort.

The largest group of foreign soldiers was the Americans, or 'GIs' as they were known from *Government Issue,* which was stamped on all their uniforms and other supplies.

I LOVE YOU, DARLING.

GIs were popular with English girls because they were paid three times as much as British soldiers, and they were very generous. They could get hold of luxuries such as cigarettes, nylon stockings and scented soap from their own Post Exchange stores and they knew the latest dance, called the jitterbug. By the end of the War at least sixty thousand English girls had become 'GI brides'.

Free French
Many Frenchmen and women fled German-occupied France. Known as the 'Free French' they fought the Nazis under the leadership of General De Gaulle.

Gurkhas
Gurkhas came from Nepal. There is still a Gurkha regiment in the British army today.

Indians
Hindu, Muslim and Sikh soldiers all fought against the Nazis.

An Australian

Australians and New Zealanders
The ANZACS, as they were known, fought bravely beside the British throughout the War.

A Handful of Heroes

The millions of men who fought in the armed forces of the Allies had some clever leaders. Here's a handful.

Dowding

Air Chief Marshal Sir Hugh 'Stuffy' Dowding was a brilliant leader of the RAF during the Battle of Britain. He was known as 'stuffy' because he lacked a sense of humour.

Eisenhower

General Dwight D. Eisenhower was the son of a poor Texan family. He was made Supreme Commander of the Allied invasion of Europe in 1944, and was so popular that in 1952 he was elected President of the USA.

Montgomery

Montgomery was a brilliant general who fought right through the War from Dunkirk to D-Day. He led the British army to victory in North Africa, before becoming commander of the British D-Day forces under Eisenhower.

Patton

General George Smith Patton was known as 'Old Blood-and-Guts' by his men. He was good at commanding fast-moving tanks and troops and led his 'Third Army' across France and into Germany in the summer of 1944.

For more information on D-Day, see page 110.

MEANWHILE - BACK IN BERLIN

NOT A NICE PLACE TO BE.

BOMBS AND MORE BOMBS

Apart from their powerful Japanese friends, and their not-so-powerful friends like Italy and Bulgaria, the Germans found themselves at war with most of the world. Life in Germany grew very tough. They had rationing and evacuations - and they had bombing.

Huge fleets of up to a thousand bombers set out from Britain to wreak destruction on German industries and cities. The British and their allies dropped millions of tons of bombs, killing many thousands of people during the War, and making more than seven million people homeless.

On 14 February 1945, in one of the worst air raids, 650,000 fire bombs were dropped on the city of Dresden, causing a fire-storm which ate up almost the entire city.

Yellow stars

If things were tough for ordinary German citizens, they were far tougher for those who did not belong to the Master Race. As early as 1941, all Jews were forced to wear a yellow star if they went out. They were rounded-up and sent to concentration camps in larger and larger numbers.

Then in 1942 the Nazis started their *Final Solution*. This was their plan to murder all the Jews they could get hold of. They built special gas chambers and furnaces in the concentration camps. More than six million Jews died.

In fact up to eleven million people may have been murdered during the Nazi *Holocaust*, not all in concentration camps. Victims included gypsies and disabled people among others, as well as Jews.

Holocaust means 'wholesale destruction'.

HIT-MEN FOR HITLER

Most Germans did not know about the Final Solution. It was not mentioned in the German newspapers or on the radio. However a handful of top officers realised that Hitler was leading his country to destruction, and they hatched several plans to kill him.

 September 1938 - plan to capture Hitler alive and declare him insane (which shouldn't have been difficult!) failed because of poor leadership.

 November 1939 - plot to kill Hitler failed because of hesitation by the plotters.

 November 1939 - another plot to kill Hitler a few days later, this time with a push-button bomb. Hitler left early and the bomb killed seven other people.

 March 1943 - plot to kill Hitler with a bomb hidden in a bottle of brandy on his private plane. The bomb failed to go off.

 March 1943 - two bombs placed in Hitler's overcoat pockets, but he didn't wear the coat.

July 1944

THE CASE OF THE MOVING BRIEFCASE

Colonel Claus Philip Schenck Graf von Stauffenberg was as brave as his name was long, and he thought Hitler was pure evil. Being a high-ranking officer he was often at meetings when Hitler was present. At one such meeting he placed a bomb with a ten-minute delay in a briefcase and put the briefcase under the table near Hitler's chair. He then left the room. Unluckily another officer moved the briefcase out of the way to the other side of a wooden support. When the bomb exploded, Hitler was protected by the wooden support - and survived. Later Stauffenberg was arrested and shot.

This was the nearest anyone came to killing Hitler - except Hitler, who eventually committed suicide.

DOODLE-BUG AGAIN!

AND WORSE ...

The quickest way to get to Germany from Britain overland is to cross the English Channel from Dover to Calais and then drive like hell through Belgium. This is fine in peacetime, but not so easy if there's a massive great Nazi army waiting for you on the other side.

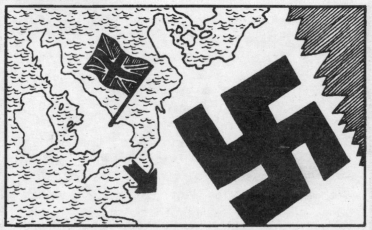

The British and their allies decided to land their armies in Normandy to the south of Calais, where German defences were slightly weaker than at Calais itself. The day of the invasion was called 'D-Day' and it was planned for 6 June 1944. The American general Dwight D. Eisenhower was put in charge.

From early that morning the sky over southern England was dark with thousands upon thousands of planes on their way to France, and the ground thundered under the wheels of countless tanks and trucks as they made their way to transport ships in the southern ports. It was the largest water-borne invasion the world had ever seen.

CROSSWORD PUZZLE

In the weeks before D-Day a number of crossword clues appeared in the Daily Telegraph. The spy-catchers of MI6 became suspicious because the solutions to the clues were secret code names.

UTAH and OMAHA were the code names for landing beaches.
NEPTUNE was the code name for the naval side of the invasion.
MULBERRY was the code name for two giant ready-made harbours which were to be towed across the Channel.
OVERLORD was the code name of the entire invasion!

The men from MI6 went to visit Leonard Dawe, the chief crossword compiler for the Daily Telegraph. Luckily for him he was able to convince them that it was all a fantastic coincidence.

The German army was smaller than the Allies', but even so the invasion could have ended in disaster had the Germans fought back more quickly. But none of the top German commanders were available to order the German forces to start fighting back:

卐 No one dared to wake Hitler till late in the morning.

卐 Rommel, back from Africa and now the German commander of Channel defences, was on a day-trip to Ulm for his wife's birthday.

卐 The commander of the tank corps in the invasion area was on a trip to Belgium.

卐 Another key German commander was with his girlfriend.

DOODLE-BUG AGAIN

Yes it's doodle-bug time again - where this book started. It was after the D-Day invasion that Hitler launched his doodle-bug flying bombs on London.

Once the Allied army had landed in Normandy it was only a matter of time before Germany was defeated. But Hitler refused to accept that he had lost the War. He boasted about a secret weapon which would turn defeat into victory. This secret weapon was the doodle-bug. On 13 June, just a week after the D-Day invasion, the first doodle-bug landed in England.

Doodle-bugs were hard to shoot down from a plane, except at close range when you might get caught in the blast. RAF pilots would fly alongside and tip a  wing beneath the doodle-bug so that it rolled out of control and crashed harmlessly.

Doodle-bugs killed six thousand people before the War was over.

Hitler had another secret weapon, the V2. This was a rocket which could fly at 5,793 kph. They killed nearly three thousand people.

The V weapons caused a second mass-evacuation from London, but they did nothing to break the British war effort. They were Hitler's last throw of the dice.

Goodbye Adolf

By April 1945 the Allies had fought their way to within a few kilometres of Hitler's Berlin headquarters, hidden in a vast concrete bunker in the centre of the city. Although defeat was staring him in the face,

Hitler could not bring himself to accept that the War was lost. As if in a dream, he spent hours playing with models of the Nazi buildings he planned to build after the War was over.

IT'S CALLED 'ADOLF HOUSE'.

WHAT A LOVELY NAME.

Finally, when the roar of guns was almost crashing in his ears, he married his long-time mistress, Eva Braun, and at around 3.30 pm on 30 April 1945 they committed suicide together in the bunker. Next day top Nazi Goebbels and his wife poisoned their six children and then killed themselves as well.

THE HORRIBLE TRUTH
The War was as good as over. But as the victorious Allies spread out over conquered Germany they were horrified to find that the Nazi empire had been far nastier than they had imagined.

They discovered the concentration camps, which were full of of starving and dead victims.

Such crimes could not go unpunished. First of all it was planned that the entire German people should suffer by being stripped of all their industries and left to live like poor farmers, but this plan, the 'Morgenthau Plan', was soon thrown out - after all, not all Germans were Nazis.

It was the Nazi leaders who had whipped up hatred of the Jews and others and caused the War in the first place. So the Allies decided to punish the German leaders - those who were still alive anyway. Following this decision there were many local trials of war-criminals, but the biggest trial was held at Nuremberg, where twenty-one top Nazis were tried and twelve were sentenced to death.

LITTLE BOY AND FAT MAN

In fact the War wasn't completely over. It was still fizzling on in the Far East, where the Japanese kept on fighting. The Japanese leaders refused to surrender even though they were losing.

The Americans decided to end the War with one almighty blow. They had been working in secret on the very first atom bomb. On 6 August 1945 *Little Boy* exploded over the Japanese city of Hiroshima.

Looking back on the cloud of dust from the explosion which rose ten thousand metres into the air, one of the American airmen described it as *'a peep into hell'*. Around 270,000 people died as a result of that one explosion.

But still the Japanese leaders would not surrender.

So on 9 August *Fat Man* was dropped on the city of Nagasaki, killing a further 87,000 people. The Japanese leaders agreed to surrender soon afterwards.

Now the War really was over.

SO WHO WON THE WAR?

WELL SOMEONE MUST HAVE.

ON THE ROAD

When the War ended, Europe was a sad sight. Many towns had been destroyed by bombs and guns, their ruined buildings stood open to the wind and rain.

On the roads more than twenty million refugees were on the move, some trying to return home, others simply moving to where they hoped they might be safe to rebuild their lives.

In the last stages of the war, the Russians had burst through the eastern defences of the once-mighty German army and had raced across Germany, at the same time as the Americans, the British and their allies had been advancing from the west. The Russians were half way across Germany when peace was declared.

And that's where the Russians stayed.

After the war was over, many of the homeless people on the roads of Europe were refugees trying to escape from the Russians, who now wanted to keep as many people as possible under their control, partly because they didn't trust the other Allies. As Churchill said later, it was as if an 'iron curtain' had been drawn across the middle of Europe. When the curtain came down, the poor people on the Russian side weren't even allowed to visit their relations on the other side.

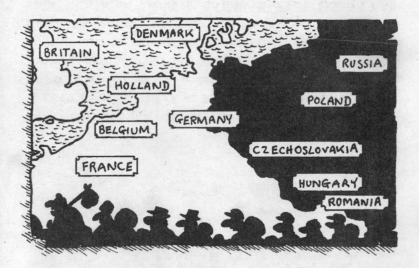

THE BIRTH OF THE BRUSSEL SPROUT
Meanwhile the Americans hatched up a scheme, called the 'Marshall Aid Plan', to lend more than a thousand million dollars to European countries, including Germany. This would help to feed the people and get industry running again.

Stalin refused Marshall Aid because of his distrust of the Americans, and life in the countries behind the Iron Curtain stayed tough for years and years. But gradually Western Europe started to grow rich and comfy again.

But would the European countries use their money to buy more guns so as to have another war in a few years time? After all, they'd had two massive great wars in just thirty one years.

Then in May 1950 the French had a brilliant idea: new weapons could not be made without coal and steel, so if countries shared control of these industries they could not make weapons without permission from each other. War between them would be impossible. The French suggested a federation to control the coal and steel industries of France, Germany and other countries of western Europe who might wish to join. The Germans were all in favour; they too had had enough of wars.

Seven years later the Coal and Steel Federation became the famous Common Market, with its headquarters at Brussels in Belgium - one of the main reasons there has been no war in western Europe since World War II ended.

THE LION LICKS ITS WOUNDS

Meanwhile, Britain after the War was like a tired old lion that's just been in a very bad fight. She had wounds everywhere and her fur was falling out. In other words: there was still rationing (it finally stopped in 1954), nearly five million people who had been in the armed forces needed to find new work, and last but not least, the Bank of England was almost out of cash.

But on the other hand, in spite of the hardship and suffering caused by the War, some good things had come out of it:

By 1943, people were better fed than they had been in the 1930s. Rationing had meant fare shares for all (well sort of) whatever their class.

Ordinary people felt that it was they who had really won the War, and not the bungling upper classes.

Women had got a taste for work and independence.

WINNIE WIN-A-LOT - OR NOT

VE Day, 8 May 1945, or 'Victory in Europe Day' to give it its full title, was Winnie's proudest day. He was mobbed by happy, singing crowds of people in the streets of London while church-bells rang and the ships in the ports hooted their sirens.

But as things turned out, although Hitler hadn't won the War, neither had Winston Churchill. In the first general election after the War, in July 1945, poor old Winnie was voted out of office, and Clement Attlee, leader of the Labour Party, became Prime Minister.

People were grateful to Churchill for leading them to victory, but he was leader of the Tory Party. Many felt that the Tories wanted to lead Britain back to the bad old days before the War, when the upper classes ruled and the poor were meant to do as they were told. The Labour Party on the other hand, promised to help ordinary people.

'THINGS I WANT TO DO' BY CLEMENT ATTLEE, LABOUR PRIME MINISTER.

The 1945 Labour Government had big ideas on how Britain should change now the War was over. They wanted to make it a better place for ordinary people:

 Nationalise the railways, the ports, the coal mines and the gas and electricity industries.

Build lots of houses for homeless people.

Start a National Health Service to provide free health care for everyone.

Make sure old age pensioners and unemployed people have enough money to live on.

If a government *nationalises* something, for instance an industry like the railways, this means the government has bought the industry, so it is now owned by the general public - the idea being that the government will run it for the good of the public not just the good of the former private owners.

WHAT WAS THE POINT OF IT ALL?

Many years have passed since the doodle-bugs fell on London. Great-Grandma and Great-Grandpa have grown old or died. The black-out curtains have long since mouldered away, and the only ration books and gas-masks you're likely to see are in museums. Just a few clues remain to remind us of that terrifying time.

 Clue No. 1 Many cities, like Coventry or Plymouth, have hardly any old buildings, because they were bombed to bits.

 Clue No. 2 We have a National Health Service and a Welfare State.

 Clue No. 3 The European Union has brought the countries of western Europe closer than they have ever been before.

 Clue No. 4 Perhaps the most important clue of all is the fact we don't live under Hitler's nightmare empire or Third Reich - the millions of people who died fighting the Nazis did not die in vain.

WORLD WAR II SURVIVORS' GUIDE

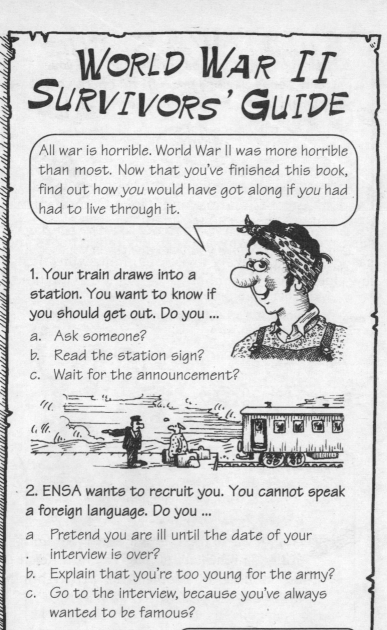

All war is horrible. World War II was more horrible than most. Now that you've finished this book, find out how *you* would have got along if *you* had had to live through it.

1. Your train draws into a station. You want to know if you should get out. Do you ...

a. Ask someone?
b. Read the station sign?
c. Wait for the announcement?

2. ENSA wants to recruit you. You cannot speak a foreign language. Do you ...

a. Pretend you are ill until the date of your interview is over?
b. Explain that you're too young for the army?
c. Go to the interview, because you've always wanted to be famous?

Continued on next page ...

3. Your family has to visit a sick aunt but your petrol ration is all used up. A friend offers to sell you some, but it's a red colour. Do you ...

a. Refuse it because the petrol's probably gone off?
b. Take it anyway?
c. Refuse because it's illegal?

4. The air raid siren has started to wail. Your dog is frightened. Before you take shelter in your local air-raid shelter, do you ...

a. Make him comfortable in the cellar?
b. Let him out to find a safe place in the garden?
c. Take him with you?

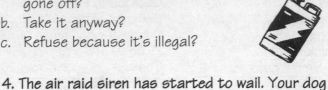

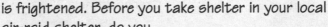

Answers

1 - **a**. The guard may shout the name of the station, but it's safest to ask someone.

2 - **c**. ENSA is the Entertainments National Service Association. Members don't fight.

3 - **c**. The police dye some black-market petrol red so as to catch the people who use it.

4 - **a**. Dogs weren't allowed in the public air-raid shelters.

INDEX

BC / ³/₁₄

WHAT THEY DON'T TELL YOU ABOUT...

ABOUT THE AUTHOR

Bob Fowke is a prize-winning children's author. He has written (or co-written) over seventy exciting books, from history and science to dinosaurs and spaceships . Bob started off painting book covers for science-fiction and horror stories by famous writers such as HP Lovecraft and Philip K Dick.

Bob is now the editorial advisor at www.youcaxton.co.uk - a company that offers support to Self-Publishers.